CONTENTS

D1455426

Published by Pleasant Company Publications Incorporated
© Copyright 1994 by Pleasant Company Incorporated

First Edition.
Printed in the United States of America.
94 95 96 97 98 99 WCR 10 9 8 7 6 5 4 3 2 1

PICTURE CREDITS
The following organizations have generously given
permission to reprint illustrations in this book:
Pages 1, 11, 13—Colonial Williamsburg Foundation;
3—Harvard Theatre Collection.

SPECIAL THANKS TO
Alison Babusci
Gregory Brumfield
Rachel Nordberg
Sam Leaton Sebesta
Lynda Sharpe and her daughter Jennifer Sharpe

NOTE: *Tea for Felicity* may be performed without royalty payments by young people at home and
school and by nonprofit organizations, provided that no admission is charged. All other rights,
including professional, amateur (other than described above), motion picture, recitation, lecturing,
performance, public reading, radio broadcasting, and television performing rights, are strictly
reserved. Inquiries about rights should be addressed to: Book Editor, Pleasant Company Publications
Incorporated, 8400 Fairway Place, P.O. Box 620998, Middleton, WI 53562.

Play Adapted by Valerie Tripp from *Felicity Learns a Lesson,* by Valerie Tripp.

Director's Guide Written by Harriet Brown and Tamara England
Edited by Tamara England and Roberta Johnson
Art Directed and Designed by Craig Smith and Jane S. Varda
Playbill Designed by Kathleen A. Brown
Produced by Karen Bennett, Laura Paulini, and Pat Tuchscherer
Cover Illustration by Dan Andreasen
Inside Illustrations by Dan Andreasen, Geri Strigenz Bourget,
Renée Graef, George Sebok, and Jane S. Varda
Historical and Picture Research by Rebecca Sample Bernstein,
Tamara England, Patti Sinclair, and Doreen Smith

Library of Congress Cataloging-in-Publication Data

Tripp, Valerie, 1951–
Felicity's theater kit : a play about Felicity for you and your friends to perform. — 1st ed.
p. cm. — (The American girls collection. American girls pastimes)
"Play adapted by Valerie Tripp from Felicity learns a lesson, by Valerie Tripp"—Verso t.p.
"Felicity 1774"—
Summary: Shortly before the Revolutionary War, nine-year-old Felicity,
who lives in Williamsburg, is torn between supporting the tariff-induced tea boycott
and saving her friendship with Elizabeth, a young loyalist from England.

ISBN 1-56247-122-8 (pbk.)
1. Children's plays—Presentation, etc. 2. Theater—Production and direction.
3. Children's plays, American. [1. Friendship—Drama.
2. Virginia—Social life and customs—ca. 1600–1775—Drama. 3. Plays.]
I. Tripp, Valerie, 1951– Felicity learns a lesson. II. Title. III. Series.
PN3157.T745   1994   792.9'2—dc20   94-28340   CIP   AC

INTRODUCTION

Felicity Merriman was a spunky nine-year-old girl growing up in Williamsburg, Virginia, just before the American Revolution. Like the other colonists, Felicity and her family had always been ruled by the King of England. But in 1774, things were beginning to change. Many people, called *Patriots*, wanted independence from the king. Colonists called *Loyalists* supported the king's rule. At the same time that the Patriots were struggling for independence, so was Felicity. *Tea for Felicity* tells the story of Felicity's desire to become independent while remaining loyal to her family, her friends, and herself.

You and your friends might enjoy putting on a play for fun, but wealthy colonial girls didn't have many chances for such amusements. They spent their time learning to manage a household and practicing gentlewomen's skills, such as fine stitchery and penmanship and the art of serving tea.

The theater in Williamsburg showed English plays, such as those by Shakespeare, but few children went to these plays. In 1774, though, all plays and public amusements stopped because the colonies were preparing for war with England. It was years before anyone in the colonies saw a play again.

FELICITY ❧ 1774

In 1774, many American colonists were struggling for independence from England. Felicity was struggling for independence, too—while trying to remain loyal to her family and friends.

These two English girls are using a Greek mask to pretend they are actors, just as Felicity and Elizabeth might have done in 1774.

Learning about Felicity's struggle for independence will help you imagine what it was like to grow up in Felicity's time. Performing this play for your friends and family will help bring history alive for you and your audience today.

PLANNING THE PLAY

PLANNING THE PLAY

1. *Choose roles and jobs.*

2. *Decide what kind of production you'll have: With or without costumes? Lines memorized or not?*

3. *Plan the action and rehearse.*

4. *Make or find sets, props, and costumes.*

5. *Make a playbill, programs, and tickets.*

6. *Have a dress rehearsal, if you'd like.*

7. *Perform the play!*

PLAY SUMMARY

The play takes place in the fall of 1774, in Williamsburg. Felicity Merriman has begun lessons in fine stitchery and the proper way to serve tea. There Felicity meets Elizabeth and her sister Annabelle, who have recently arrived from England. Felicity and Elizabeth quickly become good friends.

But changes are in the air. To protest the rule of the King of England, Felicity's father refuses to buy, sell, or drink tea. But Elizabeth's family supports the rule of the king. Felicity must find a way to remain loyal to her father yet continue her friendship with Elizabeth and the lessons she has come to love.

PARTS TO PLAY AND JOBS TO DO

There are six characters in Felicity's play, but as few as four actors can put on the play if some people take more than one part. The four **Play Scripts** in this kit include all the parts, and actors can share script books.

But it takes more than just actors to put on a play! Invite other friends to help as *stagehands* or *ushers*. Stagehands create sets and props and move scenery around during the performance, and ushers take tickets and lead the audience to their seats.

This **Director's Guide** gives you many ideas for planning and putting on the play. It has tips for making and finding costumes and props. It will help you and your friends decide which parts to play, who will do what jobs, and how to get the jobs done.

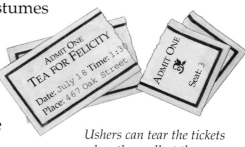

Ushers can tear the tickets when they collect them.

STAGING THE PLAY

You can make your production of *Tea for Felicity* as simple or as elaborate as you'd like. You can decide if actors should read their lines or memorize them. You can act out the play on a real stage or in a living room. The sets can be plain or fancy. You can perform for an audience or just for yourselves, with no audience. Look for ideas about stage sets, costumes, and props in the other sections of this book.

PLAYBILL AND PROGRAMS

Use the playbill poster in the back of this book to advertise your play. You can also make programs and tickets like those on page 15. Playbills and programs tell the names of the actors and the parts acted by everyone in the play. They list the director's name and the names of all the people who helped with costumes, props, and scenery. Ushers can give out programs as they take tickets and lead the audience to their seats.

BREAK A LEG!

Keep your playbill and a copy of your program to help you remember your performance of *Tea for Felicity*. Many actors keep a *play box* in which they store props and costumes. You can start your own play box and add to it each time you are in a play, just as professional actors do.

It's bad luck to say "Good luck" to anyone going onstage. Instead, say "Break a leg." And at the end of the show, don't forget the curtain call! It's your chance to bow and curtsy while the audience claps.

LENGTH OF THE PLAY

Tea for Felicity can be performed in about 20 minutes. You can also have a 10-minute **intermission**, or break, between Act Two and Act Three.

THEATER PLAYBILL

*This playbill announced a performance of Shakespeare's play **The Merchant of Venice** at the theater in Williamsburg. There is a picture of the Williamsburg theater on page 11. And Mrs. Hallam, one of the actors listed on this playbill, is shown on page 13 acting in another play!*

THE CHARACTERS

HOW TO BECOME YOUR CHARACTER

Close your eyes and imagine that you are your character. Then practice walking, talking, and moving as you think your character would.

Your imagination is your best tool for a successful performance. If you don't have a stage or elaborate props and costumes, act as if you do!

FELICITY   **ELIZABETH**

MISS MANDERLY

There are six characters in Felicity's play. But you can put on the play with just four people if one actor takes the parts of Annabelle and Father and another actor takes the parts of Miss Manderly and the Angry Man.

Don't worry about finding actors who look exactly like the pictures of the characters. Good acting will turn actors into believable characters no matter what they look like!

FELICITY is a spunky nine-year-old girl growing up in the American colonies. Felicity speaks enthusiastically, and her movements are quick—too quick, at times, to be ladylike. She is torn between her duty to her parents and her own growing need for independence.

ELIZABETH is a shy nine-year-old girl from an English family who becomes Felicity's best friend. Elizabeth wants to be a good friend to Felicity, but she's afraid of her bossy older sister Annabelle. At the beginning of the play, she looks away whenever Annabelle speaks, but by the end, she looks Annabelle in the eye.

MISS MANDERLY is a gentlewoman who gives lessons in ladylike behavior. She stands up straight, with excellent posture and a ready smile. She is warm and loving to the girls, but she will not put up with rudeness or intolerance.

ANNABELLE is Elizabeth's snobby older sister. She bosses Elizabeth and Felicity in private and acts sweet to them when Miss Manderly is nearby. She speaks in a loud, smug voice, as if she would drown out anyone else who might want to talk.

ANNABELLE

FATHER is Felicity's father, who owns one of the finest stores in Williamsburg. Father believes that people should do what they feel is right, even if it seems wrong to others. He is loving to Felicity and understands that she must find her own answers.

The **ANGRY MAN** is upset with Father and the other colonists who want independence. He speaks in a loud, angry voice, and does not really listen to Father or anyone else.

FATHER   **ANGRY MAN**

OTHER JOBS

There are many behind-the-scenes jobs in every play. Decide with your friends who will play which character, who will be the director, and who will make costumes, props, and sets. Actors can also help out as stagehands.

Stagehands who move scenery will be less noticeable if they wear dark pants and shirts.

If the actors memorize their lines, you may need a *prompter*. The prompter follows the play in a script book and whispers lines from offstage if an actor forgets them.

At the end of your performance, make sure that everyone who helped put on the show takes a bow at the curtain call!

IF YOU FORGET YOUR LINES . . .

*If you forget your lines and can't hear the prompter, just think about what your character would say and then **ad lib** (say it in your own words).*

THE DIRECTOR

Plays are exciting because lots of people work together to make them happen. But it's usually helpful to have one person be the director. The director is the person who is in charge of the play. That doesn't mean that she is the boss. The director needs to listen to other people's ideas about what should happen onstage. The more the director listens to everyone's ideas, the better the play will be.

GETTING INTO CHARACTER

One of your most important jobs as the director is to help an actor "get into character" by helping her

Felicity is upset when Annabelle accuses all colonists of being hot-headed and ungrateful.

imagine what it would be like to truly be that character. What words describe the character? How would the character show joy or anger? For example, would she stamp her foot in anger? Would she hide her face in sorrow?

You can also encourage the actor to practice walking and talking as the character would. How would Felicity walk? How would her voice change when she is happy or sad? Asking these kinds of questions and helping the actors find answers will create a more believable performance.

DIRECTOR'S TIPS

✱ Make sure that all the actors speak clearly and loudly enough to be heard.

✱ Help the actors "get into character" by asking questions about what the character is like.

✱ Remind the actors to relax as they say their lines. Using props will help them move naturally.

✱ Plan the action so that the audience can see the actors' faces.

✱ Remind the actors not to stand between another actor and the audience.

✱ Remember to praise the actors often and to make your praise sincere and specific.

BLOCKING THE ACTION

As the director, you help the actors plan how to move onstage. This is called *blocking the action.* Blocking usually takes place during rehearsal. The Play Script sometimes tells the actors how and when to move, but it is your job to give additional directions. You also give the actors little signs, or *cues*, about when to go onstage and offstage.

When you are blocking the action, try to use the whole stage. Important action should take place near the front of the stage, close to the audience.

Actors should face the audience most of the time when they're speaking, so the audience can see the actors' faces and hear their lines. But you might sometimes ask an actor to turn away to show sadness or rejection. For example, Felicity might turn away and bury her face in her hands when she cries about Elizabeth's betrayal.

KEEPING THE PLAY MOVING

Keep the play moving by helping the actors *overlap* their lines. To overlap, an actor says her first word just as the actor before says her last word. Combine overlapping with occasional pauses to make the play more lively and natural.

PRAISING THE ACTORS

One of your most important roles as director is to praise the actors. Watch for good things that happen during rehearsals and make them part of the finished performance. The best praise is specific and sincere. Many directors keep a notebook handy so they can make notes about things to remember and praise.

MUSIC AND MOOD

Before the show and during set changes and intermission, set the mood with lute or harpsichord music from the 1700s. The librarian at your school or public library should be able to help you find the right music.

Just before the play starts, the stagehand in charge of music can **fade out** *the music by gradually lowering the volume until it can no longer be heard.*

THE STAGE

I t'll be easier to talk about how to move during the play if everyone knows how the stage is laid out. There are special terms to describe the front, back, and sides of the stage. These terms are used all around the world today, from New York to London. They are the terms that actors in Felicity's time used, too.

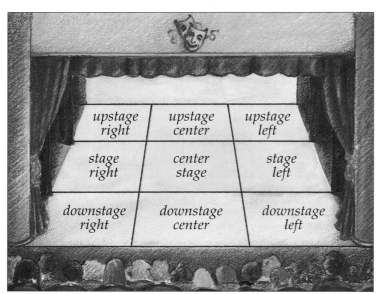

Stages used to be built on a slant, with the back part of the stage higher than the front. This angle allowed the audience to see the actors better. The terms *upstage* and *downstage* come from the way the stage slanted. *Upstage* is the area farthest from the audience—the area that used to be higher. *Downstage* is the front of the stage, nearest the audience. An actor standing in the exact middle of the stage is at *center stage*.

When an actor stands at center stage, facing the audience, the area to the actor's right is *stage right* and the area to the actor's left is *stage left*. The best way to remember *stage right* and *stage left* is to face the audience.

In a good production, you use the whole stage. The action moves around. When you block the action in *Tea for Felicity*, try to use these terms so everyone will know exactly where to move onstage.

PROPS

Props can be simple or elaborate, real or made-up. Sets can be dressed up with realistic, detailed props or with simple items that resemble the real things. Or actors can just pretend they are holding props and let the audience use its imagination!

Here are some ideas for making or finding the props in this play. Be sure to ask an adult before you use things from your home.

Use a toy tea set, so that when Felicity drops her tooth and the cups go flying, nothing gets broken. You can make a tea tray by cutting out a large circle or rectangle of cardboard and covering it with tinfoil so it looks like silver. Or use a plastic tray covered in foil. The silverware could be real, or you could use plastic spoons covered in foil. For biscuits and cakes, make real ones or use cookies or crackers on a plate.

A *sampler* is a piece of fabric with embroidered letters or shapes stitched on it. The samplers can be scraps of white or light-colored material, or squares cut from old sheets. Use a marker to draw a design on each one. Borrow embroidery hoops from your mother or another relative, or buy them at a craft or variety store.

A *petition* is a piece of paper signed by many people requesting or demanding something. Find a long piece of plain white paper and write lots of names on it so that they look like old-time signatures.

PROPS

ACT ONE
A tea set
A silver tea tray
Silverware
Biscuits & cakes

•

ACT TWO
Felicity's sampler & hoop
A petition

•

ACT THREE
Elizabeth's sampler & hoop
A tea set
A silver tea tray
Silverware
Annabelle's hat

•

ACT FOUR
Felicity's sampler & hoop

•

ACT FIVE
Both samplers & hoops
A tea set

STAGE SETS

You will need two sets for *Tea for Felicity*—Miss Manderly's parlor, and the Merriman store.

One way to create a background is by using large paper to make a mural. Light-brown paper across the back of your stage works best. You can make two separate murals—one for the parlor and one for the store—or you can make just one mural and use two sets of cutouts. If you pin or lightly tape cutouts to the mural, you can easily change them from scene to scene. For instance, you can make a cutout fireplace for Miss Manderly's parlor by drawing a fireplace on another piece of paper or cardboard and attaching it to the mural. Use paint or chalk to add details on the cutouts and mural. Applying paint with a large sponge is fast and adds texture.

Make a mirror or portraits to hang on Miss Manderly's wall by cutting oval frames out of brown construction paper. The center of the mirror can be a sheet of tinfoil, and the portraits can be pictures you've drawn yourself.

Miss Manderly's parlor.

Make the store counter out of a large cardboard box (such as a refrigerator box) set on its side. You can also make a counter by draping a dark sheet or blanket over an ironing board or several chair backs. On the mural behind the counter you can draw shelves filled with goods, such as bolts of fabric and glass jars containing cooking supplies.

The Merriman store.

CURTAINS

If you don't have a curtain that you can close
between acts, the actors can simply finish what
they are saying and exit at the end of the act.
Stagehands can quietly set the stage for the next
act. You could also have a *blackout* by
having a stagehand
turn off the lights just
before the actors leave
the stage and then turn
them back on when the

The Next Day

stage is reset. When you are ready to start the next
act, place a sign that says "Miss Manderly's Parlor"
or "The Merriman Store" on an easel or chair to tell
the audience where the new act takes place. Or a
stagehand can hold the sign. Signs can also tell
how much time has passed.

LIGHTING

Because both of the sets are indoor sets, the
lighting should be bright enough so your audience
can see everything clearly, but not so bright that it
appears as if the actors are outdoors.

WILLIAMSBURG'S FIRST THEATER

This model shows a side view of the first theater in Williamsburg, advertised in the playbill on page 3. George Washington attended plays here. In the middle of the theater, you can see a group of actors standing onstage. The large area behind the stage held many changes of scenery, backdrops, and props. The seats along the side cost the most, and the seats in the back cost the least.

COSTUMES

COSTUME TIPS

❧ The very simplest way to identify characters doesn't even require costumes! An actor can wear a sign around her neck with her character's name printed large enough for the audience to read. This way, actors can easily switch parts without having to switch costumes!

❧ Breeches can be made by putting rubber bands around the cuffs of a pair of pants and then pushing up the cuffs to just below the knee. The rubber bands will keep the cuffs in place.

Costumes help bring a play to life. They also help the audience identify the characters. Your costumes can be as simple or fancy as you want.

For an elaborate production, you could rent or borrow colonial costumes from a costume shop. Or you could make your own costumes from colonial patterns and cotton cloth.

But you don't need historical costumes to make your characters come to life. Actors can perform without costumes, or you can create costumes out of simple things in your own closet or your family's closets. Be sure to ask for permission first! And remember, the actors don't have to look like the characters to be believable. If they imagine themselves as the characters and act that way, they'll convince the audience no matter what they look like or what they're wearing.

FELICITY wears a long-sleeved jacket, a long skirt that comes to her ankles, white stockings, black shoes, and a white mob cap. Her hair is parted in the middle and tied back with a ribbon in a low ponytail. She wears a wide-brimmed straw hat that goes over her mob cap when she is outside.

ELIZABETH wears a long-sleeved gown, white stockings, and black shoes. Her hair is also pulled back in a low ponytail that is tied with a ribbon, and she can wear a pinner cap or a mob cap.

MISS MANDERLY's clothes are the same style as Elizabeth's, although the neckline of her gown may be cut slightly lower than Elizabeth's. Her hair is pinned up in the back and she wears a pinner cap on her head. She may wear a shawl wrapped around her shoulders.

ANNABELLE's clothes are fancier than Felicity's or Elizabeth's. Her gown might be made of satin or another fancy material. Instead of a mob cap, she wears a pinner cap similar to Miss Manderly's.

FATHER wears a long-sleeved white shirt, a vest, a jacket, knee breeches, white stockings, and black shoes. He may have long hair that is tied back in a ponytail and a three-cornered hat that he removes when he is inside.

The **ANGRY MAN's** clothes are the same style as Father's, but he does not remove his three-cornered hat in the store.

QUICK CHANGES

❧ *Practice making quick costume changes. The actor who plays both Annabelle and Father has to change costumes four times, so it's important for her to be able to do so quickly!*

❧ *In Acts One, Three, and Five, when the actor plays Annabelle, she can wear Father's breeches under Annabelle's long gown. For Acts Two and Four, she should quickly remove the gown and pinner cap and put on Father's vest and jacket. Quick changes will be easier if costumes are always left in the same place.*

❧ *The actor who plays both Miss Manderly and the Angry Man can also wear breeches under her gown.*

PERFORMING IN THE COLONIES

*Mrs. Nancy Hallam, acting here in Shakespeare's **Cymbeline,** was a popular actor in Felicity's time. (She is listed on the playbill shown on page 3 for her role in **The Merchant of Venice**.) Actors in colonial times often performed in the clothing they wore offstage, unless the play required unusual costumes, such as this one.*

13

MOB CAPS AND PINNER CAPS

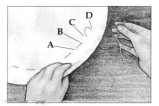

MOB CAP   *Step 1*

To sew a running stitch, come up at A and go down at B. Come up at C and go down again at D.

Step 2

Step 3

PINNER CAP

Use a running stitch to sew the lace to the fabric circle.

MOB CAPS

To make a mob cap, use a compass to draw an 18-inch circle on a large piece of paper. Cut out the circle pattern, pin it to a piece of cotton fabric, and then cut out a fabric circle. Unpin the paper pattern. Knot one end of a long piece of thread and sew a running stitch around the circle, 2 inches in from the edge (see Step 1). When you finish, cut the thread, leaving about 2 inches of loose thread at the end. Knot another long piece of thread and sew a second circle of running stitches $1/4$ inch inside the first circle of stitches. Don't cut this thread yet!

Hold the loose threads of both rows by the unknotted ends (see Step 2). Gently pull the two rows of thread until the cap is gathered enough to fit loosely on your head. Tie the threads off so the cap stays gathered. Cut off the excess thread. Finish your cap by sewing on a pretty bow (see Step 3).

PINNER CAPS

To make a pinner cap, use a compass to draw a 4-inch circle on a piece of paper. Cut out the paper circle and pin it to a piece of light cotton fabric. Then cut out the fabric circle. Unpin the paper pattern. Next you'll need $5/8$ yard of flat lace or $1/2$ yard of pre-gathered lace that is 2 inches wide. Pin the lace around the circle, gathering it gently as you pin. Use a running stitch (see Step 1 above) to sew the lace around the edge of the circle. When you come back to the place where you started, tie a knot and cut off the extra thread. Remove the pins. Use hair pins to attach the pinner cap to your head.